KU-557-859

Schools Library and Information Services
S00000718548

Flip the Flaps

Animal Homes

Judy Allen and Simon Mendez

KINGFISHER

First published 2009 by Kingfisher
an imprint of Macmillan Children's Books
a division of Macmillan Publishers Limited
The Macmillan Building, 4 Crinan Street, London N1 9XW
Basingstoke and Oxford
Associated companies throughout the world
www.panmacmillan.com

Consultant: David Burnie

ISBN 978-0-7534-1736-2

1 3 5 7 9 8 6 4 2
1TR/0309/LFG/UNTD/157MA/C

A CIP catalogue record for this book is available from the British Library.

Printed in China

Contents

Trees

A tree is a bit like a block of flats, with homes at every level. Birds and squirrels nest in the branches. Small animals live in cracks in the bark. Woodpeckers may live in a hole in the trunk.

woodpecker

1. What is a squirrel's nest like?

2. Why do woodpeckers peck wood?

3. Which small animals live in trees?

What lives on tree bark?

peppered moth

bark beetle

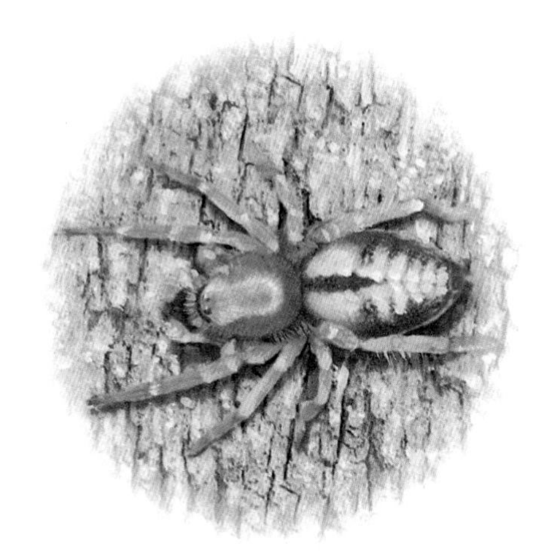
spider

Stones

Big stones are home to small animals that like to live where it is dark and damp. Lift one and you might find earwigs and woodlice, springtails and centipedes.

thrush

snail

1. No. Sometimes the den may be under a shed or dug under tree roots.

2. Yes. The female, known as a vixen, digs the den. Or she may just enlarge an old abandoned burrow.

3. Yes, lots – badgers, prairie dogs, kingfishers, bumblebees and mice all live in burrows.

Inside a prairie dog burrow

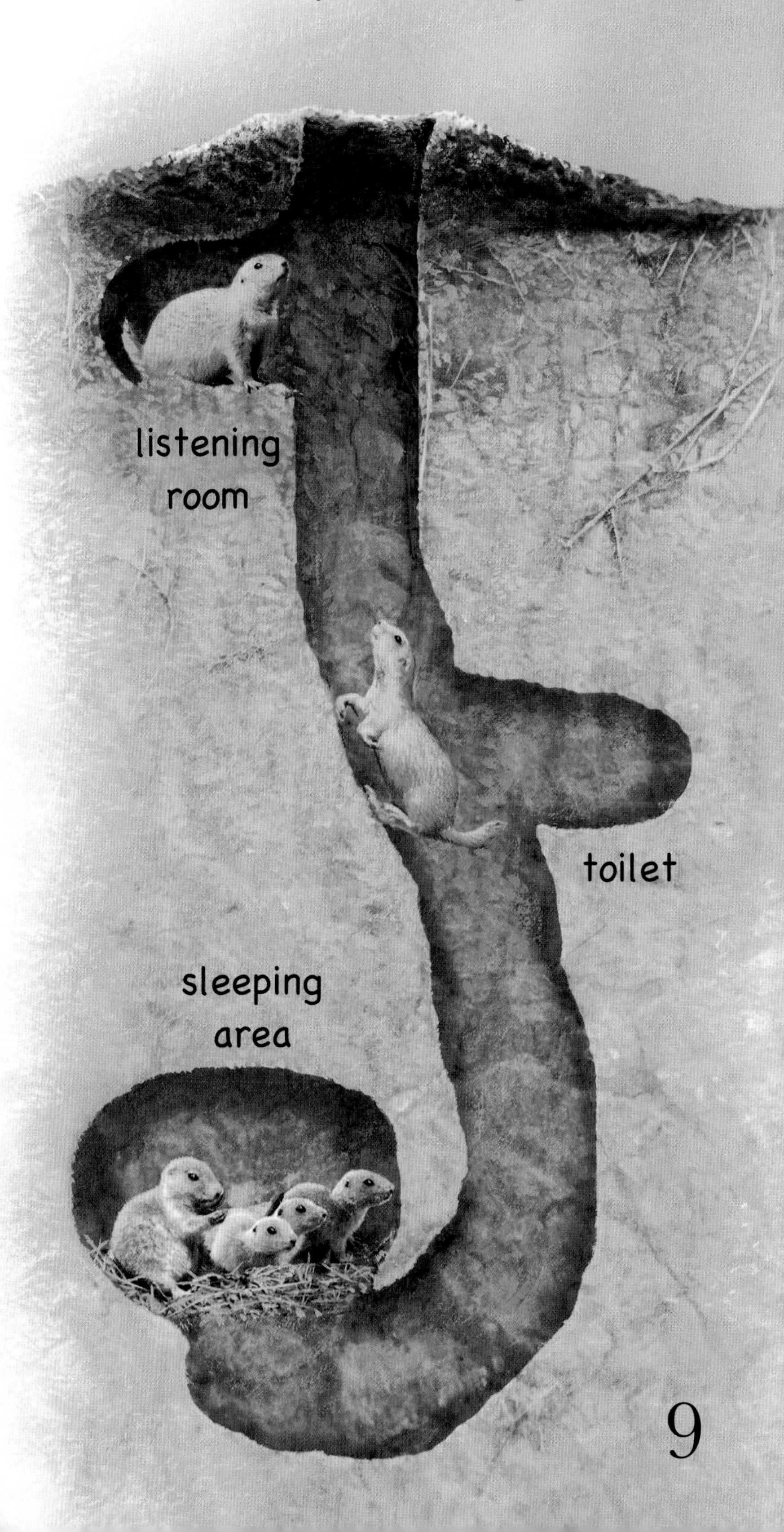

Ponds

Ponds are like tiny worlds. Dragonflies hover above, while their young live below. Water boatmen and pond skaters live at the surface. Beetles dive. Tadpoles hatch out and turn into frogs.

1. No. Tadpoles hatch from frogspawn, become froglets and climb out. Adult frogs live on land and in ponds.

2. Dragonflies lay their eggs on pond plants underwater. The young hatch and live in the pond for two years.

3. Some can. Others, like the diving beetle, take an air bubble down with them.

dragonfly young

A dragonfly young changes

Shells

Animals with shells already have homes. Some can go inside their shells and sleep safely. Only the hermit crab doesn't grow its own shell. It finds an empty one to move into.

hermit crab

Lobsters and mussels also have shells.

1. Why are the shells empty?

2. Where do hermit crabs find the empty shells?

3. Do turtles change their shells when they need bigger ones?

A snail's shell grows with it

Young snails have small, soft shells.

The shell grows bigger and harder.

Caves

There are sea caves, ice caves and land caves where bats may live. Some bats sleep in cracks, while others sleep upside down.

1. Bats sleep by day. At night, they fly out to feed.

2. Yes, it may be cold in a cave, but it is sheltered from winter wind and rain.

3. Lots of insects, and spiders and scorpions, too. They are often white if they always live in the dark.

Other animals in a bat cave

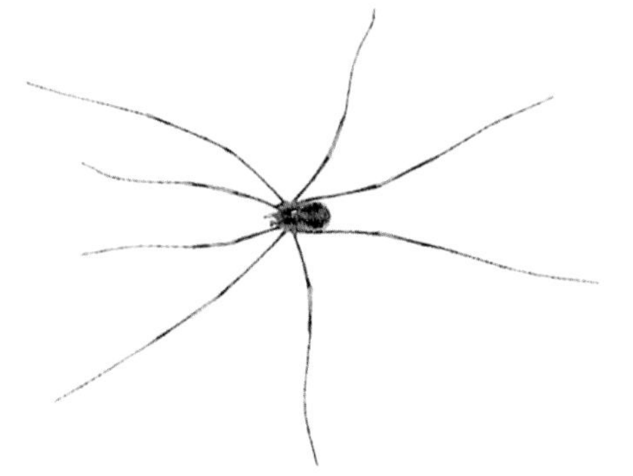

harvestman

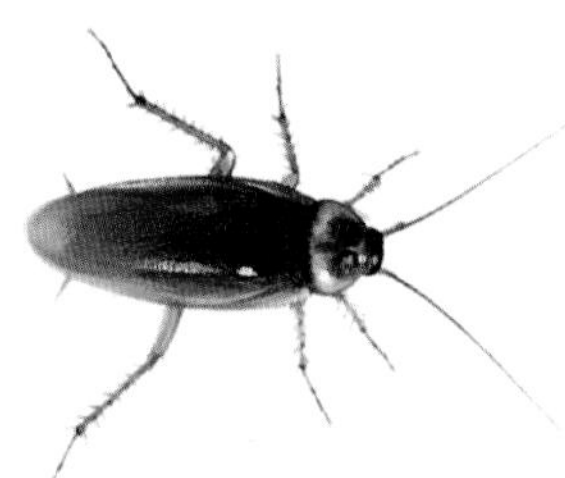

cockroach

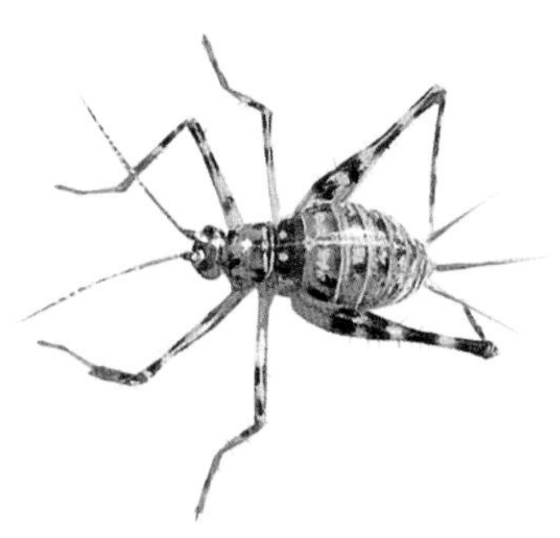

cave cricket

cave beetle

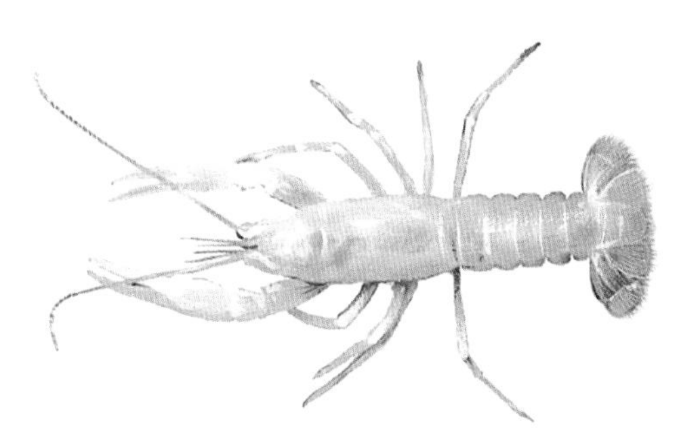

cave crayfish

Home-builders

Beavers use branches and stones to build a lodge in a river or lake. They can bite right through trees with their sharp teeth and chew the wood into useful lengths.

1. The lodge entrance is underwater.

2. No. Beavers eat plants, twigs and tree bark. They store food in the water around the lodge or in a room inside it.

3. Yes. Birds, squirrels and bees all build homes. The tailorbird makes a home by sewing leaves together.

A tailorbird builds a nest

sewing together leaf edges

safe in the nest

Index